Slavesong

Slavesong
the art of singing

Kwelismith

Anacostia Repertory Company
Washington, DC

Typeset at The Writer's Center Bethesda, Maryland

Color separation and cover Marktone Litho Services

Cover: La Maison D'Esclaves

Library of Congress Catalog Card Number 89-85170
ISBN 0-9624092-0-0

Acknowledgements:

This publication is supported in part by a fellowship grant from The DC Commission on the Arts and Humanities.

Many loving spirits aided me in labor, either as critics/editors, musicians, moral supporters or publishing advisors. Among the midwives of Slavesong are Ann T. Green, Valerie Russell, Toi Derricotte, Essex Hemphill, Alaiyo Moseley, Carol Yampolsky, Rachel Guido deVries and the Feminist Women's Writing Workshop, Jill Spisak, Joan Dickenson, Nancy Bereano, Grace Cavalieri, Regina Moore, Darla Davenport-Powell, Crystal Stephen, Regina McConnell, Leroi Dorsey and the friends who have attended/supported my readings and performances.

Dark Diva, Zora and Namibia first appeared in *Three Apples Fell.*

Photographs: cover and sections taken in Dakar, Senegal 1982

In memory of William T. Dickey and Alice Daly Dickey

Contents

the wail

in the belly

harmony

the sermon

the ring shout

melody

. . . like the nightingale, the lark, we are birds of humanity.

Slavesong

(for Tawana Brawley)

1

I feel pointed
in the direction of
extinction
I know the corridors
self-denial self-abnegation
scratching bars for release
I know the smell of
iron under fingernails
I remember the dark hole
I came out of
I know there is no difference
between the auction block
and *on the block* the
butcher block a
confused pound of pussy
waiting to be bought
the transfer
the property
the trust
a free black woman
I want to know who owns me

2

I am not pitiful
sodwoman
snaggle toothed
blank memory
dragged like dodo
across plain states
I am not sapphire/ruby
just another pissed off
black woman sour
lips hand on hip
skillet of hot grits
lay in wait for her
no good man

nor licentious
sado masochistic monster
waiting to fuck the strap
off some overseers whip
I am not sorry
I have been processed
homogenized deodorized
polished stone
that glows in white
light

3

only fifteen years old
I am despised
and rejected sliced
open by six white men
boned   gutted   bloated
into a hefty bag their
fecal matter smeared
through my hair
a tomb beyond insane
I dissolve
Tawana
a garbled sound
signifying
nothing

4

come tender night
blanket my scars
in a shrill silence
stars drop
invisible chains
my hair screams
against
dark mornings
generations arms
rolled above head
pulled from sockets

breasts hang from
skin strings
dripping
blood and milk
a metronome
marking centuries

the art of singing

1

in senegal
they ask how we
wail from deep
in the belly

first I say
oh
we cry out the blood
the lungs
bellow in tall waves
the bones remember the
hundred million
eyes lighting the atlantic

2

then I say
exactly
I reach back beneath
the lilac tree that
bloomed beside the porch
by the kitchen

the lilacs took the air
like a cathedral organ

I cut branches to smell
inside the house with coffee
bacon eggs and momma and daddy's
early morning duo
her splat tat tat tat and his
low boooop oops 'scuse me

I reach back to the grave marker
discarded beside the porch
billy 1936-1950
I thought they
buried him there

I would lean over the railing
stare at the stone   numb
my tongue twisted like
the cornrows on my head unable
to form the air to question death

3

what made it so crazy
the big black vacuum cleaner
swelling to suction
dusty little dark girls

the roller coaster ride down
dickey's hill in a baby stroller
billy pushing 30 miles an hour
let go to enjoy my terror

past chain link fences
plaqued mad dog slobbering
great danes rabid boxers
barking trembling ground

4

what was a 6 year old
floating up to her elbows
in cold greasy dish water
for 12 people at 12 o'clock
midnight wearing one plastic
shoe

lazy little cindyella

now I lay me down to sleep
I pray the lord my soul to keep

in bed the shadows danced
the flowered wall paper the big
iron lung stood over me frozen
pointed his thick finger
called me polio rubbed his hollow
chest called me tb

for one year
I slept on clean white sheets
ate clean white food
saw clean white nurses
clean white doctors
swallowed clean white medicine
wheeled the chair to a
clean white schoolroom
listened to bible stories
from ancient blue white ladies
sang good night sweetheart
with the mcguire sisters

5

back home
I slept between them
hot and cold they didn't
like me contagious   I didn't
like them either hot and cold
love and hate knives and forks
far away blue and dark

I remember that
father daughter shoe race
he took my 6 year old shoes
ran relay with the other fathers
to get the right shoes
back on the right kid
before the bell

I did not want that
kind of wooden father
pretending to like
what he hated

I needed more his music his
finger's tremolo on the violin
moving air for g string
the beauty aching in his gut

6.

mean and jumpy
what made fathers
carry a black metal lunchbox
mean and jumpy
eat hot tamales and sardines
yell at kids hate company
sweat and sway the conductor's
thumb backwards until we sang perfect
tell me the stories of jesus

make us do saturday chores to
texaco opera broadcasts
hate gutbucket
be stingy giving quarters
be lonely cutting grass
be wrong beaten model t ford
be angry and jumpy and sad

7

ring
mulberry 14588
momma holiness
daddy methodist
grandma baptist
I craved fast music
baptized rock gospel
juniorchoir pat clap sway
pizza rehearsals
winter taffy pulls hayrides
midnight skate friedchicken summers

I wished momma would make everybody
wash their own plate so washing
dishes wouldn't be nobody's job

but she got us up at
3 am to sweep crumbs from
under the kitchen table

hands on hips eyes flashing
girl you aint swept this floor
was it your turn to do dishes

8

momma smothered us between her thighs
to comb our hair   she used hair rep
on our hair I wanted dixie peach or
royal crown to smell black like my
friends evelyn and margaret
hair rep didn't have no smell

microscope glasses
made eyes look like peas
peas and pimples made
everything all knotted
pulled the head down

walked ten paces behind girlfriends
wished mirrors opaque

let the chickens
walk on my hair rep

9

in june I could not sleep
charged
I rose with the dew
to smell morning creep in
bobwhites bluejays
wet roses and honey suckle

picnic   the zoo   picnic
burnett woods slide the
cement slide down down
up up down again thump and jump
sweat and kool-aid popsicles
potato salad fun and sun
sing and hum

momma unveiled her long
brown breast to feed
the new yellow baby
pretty fat yellow baby

the kids teased titty bump
titty bump tit tit titty bump
yo momma

10

I reach back beneath
the lilac tree that
bloomed beside the porch
by the kitchen

the lilacs took the air
like a summer saxophone

I cut branches to smell
inside the house where
violet sweated
wild turkey   mind
missing days   body missing months
she banged her shadow against
the moon
staggered the
flowered wall paper dark

I loves you porgy
please don let em take me

her mandarin alto
riding the waves

matching
nina simone

stride for stride

Ain Nonnie Poems

prologue

well suh

yes indeedy

served mah brockli souflay
week fo lass
fo de rosenbergs party
now de whitfields
want me down in
springfield fo mah
rolls an german chocolate cake

yes indeedy

gonna be a mighty big one
forty fifty sixty folks or moah
course you know
ah need a
touch up
round mah edges
fo ah even walk thru
miss harriettes doah

1953

amazing grace

alice tell em
chilren te git
somwhea n sidown
bedda cut de tv
off too

a thunder storm
slices dark sky
at mid day
Ain Nonnie
slides her buttermilk
hips into mommas
beauty shop chair
closes her jesus
lovin eyes tight
squeezes her witefolk
lovin hands

yall stop dat
gigglin   doncha
hyea de lawd talkin

she spreads her
deep face chained
to hot greasy stoves
gaps her vericose legs
trained to back doors

amazing grace how sweet
the sound that saved
a wretch like me

her voice
rich
like alabama earth
booms against the
lightening
singin up
roots to claim
gods storm

ah once wuz loss
but now ahm found
wuz blind but now ah see

1959

gone with the wind

ain nonnie
the best cook
in cincinnati
she proud as
new money
workin for the
oharas in
her stainless steel
kitchen in their
thirtytwo room
georgian colonial

she got me
baby sittin job
watchin melanie
and charlie
while miss scarlet
lounged in and
out of the
master suite
all day with
rhett butler

i was proud
to be workin
for the oharas
sleepin in the
maids quarters
brushin bathin
feedin melanie
and charlie
feelin sorri
for miss scarlet
when the laundress
didn show up

i was proud
glidin up and down
our spiral staircase
until

ain nonnie said
i was spose to use
the back stairs
until
ain nonnie got
mad at me   for slappin
charlie cause he
spit on me

1962

seventeen

bored
american history
maps and lines
angles charters
states rights
no negroes
rights
no women
white
bald-headed
pot-bellied men

friday and saturday night
i do the hot grind
redlight basement parties
drink gin

no boyfriend
i sing
jesus lover of my soul
sunday
so in love monday with
music and english and gym

i see ain nonnie on the bus
i ease next to her on
a quarter of the seat

seventytwo today
got me a boyfriend
since mr smith don gone

she chuckles as she leans
in to me not caring
whether anyone else hears
her or not

yes indeedy
keeps me a boyfriend

you think boyfriends
is just for young folks
well ahm young
seventytwo years young

seventeen years old
ain nonnie wearin
new love like a
easter hat at her age

i rush home
to tell my sister
how crazy
ain nonnie is

epilogue

ain nonnie lived in a poor place herself
charcoal brown a mammy   how she laughed
gold frame glasses polished on the tip
of her nose   head bobbing up and down steady talking

yes suh
dey say ahm a fine cook
an ahm proud of it
yes indeedy
ah run my hands over de
smoove stainless steel stove
an ahm happy   dey respec me hyeah
ah have run of de house
silvie de maid
de laundress virginia
sam de gardener   de nurse do what
ah tell 'em   an yes suh ah run de
butler's pantry too
ah have mah suite off
de kitchen an so foth   course
mah lil ole room back home wid
uncle tom   ummhumm mah
ole greycouch mah pots n pans
mah castiron skillet   ain much but its
mine   ummhumm   yes suh been cookin
since ah wuz toteen yeahs ole
down in huntsville alabama   cook
fo de wilsons   part cherokee
ummhumm they wuz my motha's
people   nevah earned a dime
tho   they like mah singin
useta cook n sang
put mah soul in it
close mah eyes tho mah
head back

ain nonnie let people have a piece of her
she put her foot up on a rock in the kitchen
made petrified biscuts dream in your mouth
rich whitefolks ate her up like they eat up
the best of everything

neckbones n sauerkraut

twenty-two nutmeg arms
reach for the pot

pass the pot
clockwise

first daddy's
big bass hands
then
round the table
down to
me

one lone neckbone
a few strands of
kraut

pass the
hot sauce

suck the last bone
suck the milk from
the last bone
suck the last love bone
down like
momma's
breast

Cincinnati: A Painting

I think of painting
a forest of colors where I was born
purple blackberries mashed between
cobblestones   mossgreen shade
hung over damp treebark
sticks of brown underbrush
the smooth wind summer rain
and garbage behind the
cincinnati waterworks
the meyer meat packing co.

What wide street was that
where factory soot painted
orange buses black   the smell of pig
flesh burned the air   the
greasy squeals led to slaughter.

Inside the packing house
mostly white packers wore white coats
ran machines heaved bacon slabs
shook weiners.

A fly in the buttermilk
I heard the gathered talk
redneck stories

Why the women grew leather faced
why they liked gold teeth
and cussed out of the side of their mouths
how Anna had to drop out
of school because she had
no clothes to wear why
Buzzy and Goldie were
lovers   their fathers
had no shame about flipping
their penises into their mouths
or their baby's mouths when the
pacifier got lost, how now their
toddlers reach to grandpas cock
for comfort.

My hair a shock of wool shooting
out from under my dustcap
Georgia yells across the room
maybe you oughta smear a lil a this
bacon grease on your hair.

Dark Diva

for Buford Bryant

Singers plotting to take over
the met, we shaped vowels dark
spit consonants through
full ruby lips laid tracks

In old italian/ german leider
you were richard tucker
I was grace bumbry.

My ears burned cold when
those green eyes snapped tossing
me that scrubrag for a costume.

He would not let my darkskinned
hands even brush the velvet cape
I asked for. I yanked the rag from him,
ran to the library eyes hot and watery,

Look everybody! look at what the
green-eyed sonofabitch swears is good
enough for a nigger to wear when she
portrays an egyptian princess!

Maids and cooks heard about the
scrubrag   brought their wigs,
rhinestones, satin, brocade and lace.

I was amneris, you radames, *
egypt in ethiopia   glory to isis
sing rage eat fire sable princess
a slave with a crown is a queen.

We melted bars from tradition
sprinkled chimes on stage
saw trumpets pierce blue eyes
hands applaud like rain,

The magical menacing dream.

* characters in the opera Aida

the moan

Sometimes the flight is long between possible landings . . .

Sometimes I unzip
this black jacket throw back run
tissue flapping veins

Dropout

a summer youth employee

smirk across
lips
he snickers
scratches his
pen
up
down
paper
laughs
distracting
other students
yawns
balls up paper
demands permission
to join
the men
on the
corner

graffiti

elementary school girl's john

I hate
you
beche
I hate
you to
and
who aver rote
this is
motherfuck
bich
Look at
my duck
dick
kiss
my
ass

A round peg over a square hole

I walk backwards away
from myself into
stiff brown chairs
chalk dust over
my fingers over my art
a round peg over a square hole,

My teaching too black
for the system
I keep trying to bolt it back
teach the children a tomato dance
teach french pearcoring
teach appalachian humming.

I walk past myself out of
fear and habit into
prison walls
painted wardens
stabbing air with letter openers
sloshing bull whips guarding
me from myself,

Keep the niggers in line
trash independent thinking
reward conformity, teaching
black children to read is still
against the law punishable by
social isolation and a lowered
performance rating,
teach em to be
good gluttonous consumers
sing all praises due
i magnin, neiman marcus,
saks 5th avenue
limit that
black pride stuff to february.

Take the money girl! just keep movin
you been teachin long enough
do it by rote go on in there
an git that check they owe you that.
it's dirty money. hell! you crazy!

The length of the lights makes me dizzy
I suffocate from sand feet
pounding toward my room, sugar brown
faces, the adolescent crust layered
in baby fat, the chubby fingers kneading
tugging pulling   come on pleaze.

Most wardens
are light skinned
some darker tones have
risen the ranks   light or dark
brainless wonders rule the roost.

You like to teach all that
thinking stuff. I want em quiet
they're too noisy.

Fuck her!   smile talking angry
to myself   a mad woman   no
a round peg over a square hole

The customs, the cross
the nomenclature/ CBC
crush black children
designed to fail   the grim
nasty links, the barbedwire

I like to teach the song
It's alright to cry
I never do I'm empty

For years
I crawled between
cracks for fresh lilacs
wild berries and freely gave from my catch

For years
I rode the schedule
the stinking train on the skinny track
the death track starched manners
peroxide, wooden corsets swimming
in pork fat earmarked self-destruction,

Now eight-thirty gets later and later
I remove the shackles
unfasten the helmet, the yoke
the collar and inch off
this trained slave toward myself.

rope rhyme

ten twenty thirty forty
fifty sixty seventy eighty
ninty one ten twenty thirty
forty . . .

gone.

in the street
somebody's brother
mother/ is peddling dope /
lined up waiting for the coke hand.

I hear gunshots
I hear them easier now
I don't get up to look outside
it is background   it is vapor
it is mist.

I don't know enough about
wild death.

No

I don't know
the 13 14 15 yr old
dope dead murdered.
48 thousand pounds of tender black
flesh spoiled this year
part of
the dough of society kneaded in
like the starspangled banner
you know
sung in the key of
rhinestone bmw's and children
beeperkeepers.

even
3 & 4 year olds know how to
make crack   they've seen
grandma crush the rock
cook it up   seen momma
shrivel up shootin up   they've
seen death eyes lying on the
bathroom floor at night

you know
the light
for children who are afraid
they step over
lift the lid
and pee.

they know junior needs the money
troopers   reeboks   boombox
they know the family
needs the buzz needs the high
needs the game

they know the crack houses
the cop dealers   the car dealers
the dealer's dealer it's a job
the main artery of life
death.

I don't hear gun shots
anymore. I hear the missing
street chants the rope rhymes
the slap of double dutch
feet skipping pavement.

ten twenty thirty forty fifty
sixty seventy eighty ninety one
ten twenty thirty forty . . .

gone

a child speaks

I laugh
when they interrupt
jeopardy
talkin bout

special news report

say no to drougs
reefa keels brain sails
cocaine is addictive
deaf by o d
drougs keel

even the camera man
be high

I laugh

when they interrupt
all my children
talkin bout

special news report

stop babies from
havin babies
public schools
mus sail condoms
birf control peels

I laugh

ain't no public schools
on birf control
a school is a school
a docta is a docta
a school is not no docta

I laugh and laugh

say no to drougs
reefa keels brain sails
cocaine is addictive
deaf by o d
drougs keel

I laaauuugh

marion barry is mayor
julian bond is brilliant
richard pryor is rich
len bias is dead

three out of four is good

I laugh and laugh and laugh
I might be pregnant
but least I be wise

Simply Luvly

Karon dead
how Karon dead
tell u de truf
ah don rememba

ah got busted on
narcotic and manslaughter

ah went ovah Karon house
roun bou tin aclock saddy nite
we wuz gon hang out
at dis club on kennilworf
ah we ah mean ah bought sum
vakka n Karon had sum weed
ah had smoke two jaints
wile she wuz gitin ready

roun bou twelve aclock deaz two dude
came ovah   one call peacock
cause he wear alla deaz loud
hawaian lookin shirt
de uvuh one ah on rememba
he jus sit n stare
reel quiet you know like
he on harly say nuffin

wel peacock wint back in de
bedroom wit Karon n ah wuz
sitin on ne couch watchin tv
de quiet one tuk out his
sringe n stuff n starded
shootin up ah gues afta dat he
stard acckin reel chummy
he say he have sumpin else
do I won't sum ah say it
dependon what it is
he git up n go lisen at
Karon bedroom te see if
dey cummin   he take
sum luvly out say he
stole it outta peacock pouch
he scared a peacock   ah wuz
gittin kinna bored so yeah
ah did de boat wid em

nex teng ah hear sumpin
like somebodie chokin n gagin
de room keep turnin look
like peacock shirt eveywhea
ah cain harly breeve
its sumpin hevy on me
ah feel cole n sweady
feel sumpin sharp ter
into me ah cain harly
breeve ah cain muv sumpin
reel hevy weighin on me
terin me apart

ah scream for Devon n Markie
ah rememba ah lef dem sleep

Devon n Markie mah son
aight n twelve
ah don see Karon nowhea

musta been de nex day
de polices kick in Karon
do ah wuz on de couch
all cole n brown nekked
de brown couch wuz blood
stains on it de sringe
still on de end table
n cigarett papas n traces
a powda

de polices jus slip dem
cole handcuffs on me still
nekked dey put mah coat roun
me n led me

dey talkin on de polices radio
bout a homicide

ah godda call Devon n Markie
pleaze leme call
mah son no ah don have no
atturny ah don need no
dam atturny

Karon dead?
tell u de truf
ah don rememba

rhythm

I take back the drum, I walk on goatskin rhythms . . .

Jazzjam

for Shirley Horn

Sheee
bass it up
call drum
to take it away
give it back
lay it down
loww
swing fingers
slice
ivory bright moments
walk it down town
turn it around
run it home
backwards

stop

wrap
her lips
round midnight
niicce an eaassy
call me back
to witness
my birth
3 times
Her
Majesty

ahhhh

She messwithit
niicce
like
Sassy *

* Sarah Vaughan

Ma Rainey News

She put it right there for me
But I was too blind to see
She put it right there for me
But I was too blind to see
Ma Rainey been trying to tell me
Since nineteen twentythree

Well she told me
Bout them all night long blues
Yeah she told me
Bout them all night long blues
Come sixty years later
Still the same old news

Ain't nobody gonna treat
A good woman right
Ain't nobody gonna treat
A good woman right
The kinder she is
The more she gon have to fight

My baby don want me
Left me out here on my own
Said my baby don want me
Left me out here on my own
Broke my heart
In a lowdown dirty lovestorm

Well I don know
When my luck will change
Said I don't know
When my luck will change
But I done learned my lesson
Ain't gon trust no man again

She put it right there for me
But I was too blind to see
She put it right there for me
But I was too blind to see
Ma Rainey been trying to tell me
Since nineteen twentythree

doin it in the park

Dorothy Donnegan

patent leather piano under lavender lights
gold grass roseblack night I am here to listen
hear how the imagination explains white keys
hammer strings roaring black bass

she enters

throw her legs around the
six foot six and pump   chile
do you hear do you see
she make love
make collard greens
and blackeyed peas
shut my mouth got me slobbin like a fool
say what   the piano cookin   somebody
make that girl behave she
in the kitchen fixin mixin stirrin
up a orchestra in her fingers
drums in her head in her butt cymbals
church between her legs make liberace
look like tofu

one do not tell about miss dd
one must experience her
pointin out the trumpet
praisin humble
steppin struttin cuttin
legs poppin like corn
serious business no mistake
sistah do not miss nothin
take 5 take 6
sequined swishtail back
twinkle twinkle little star
you don't wanna do nothin do you
take the A train lefthand
roll bass pose then leanback
dahling funkin up the top
jugglin ice cubes on the right
make everybody disappear

miss blue lady
miss medicine band lady
center stage star under stars lady
in this grape august wind
you scramble my mind
knock me past where
I woulda been
tomorrow grab me
in the heart of center
where ghost choirs clang

May morning

in the morning
may morning
downside up
mushrooms
brown edges
vinaigrette
natural juice
strawberries
fat succulent
fold beneath fold
to blow in
hole after hole
harmonica season
new orleans
bourbon street sweet
old contemporary
sliced honeydew
dripping liquid sounds
cupped in
brown hands
suck fruit sounds
into teeth
breathless
shallow breather
O Oh! OH!!

GGOOODDD
DAMN!

no more
long tunes or
short mornings
may strawberries
mushrooms or
honeydew harmonicas
on
bourbon street

Dancer

For Nina Montgomery

How we fall between
the cracks of difference
depends on the distance
we need to keep from ourselves

your face
a benin mask
stretched and patched
by fire and plastic surgery

your head
thrown back
breasts arched forward
announce your arrival

I watch you
walk on water
your long taut
limbs embrace the sun

dance designs
on my senses
you are monk
you are mingus

you offer me your hand
I hesitate
my clay eyes trace
the contours of your scars

your hands are not whole
I was always told
it is impolite to stare
I want to understand your hands

I want to know
how you were burned
if you still feel pain

you laugh easy from your
ribs

I weigh my need
for understanding
on your scale
of self-acceptance

I am not steady
I squeeze your hand
kiss your cheek for
reassurance

improvisation on pussy

snap crackle pop
pussy
born to serve
born to serve

snap crackle pop
pussy
born to serve
born to serve

townhouse
split level
ranch
electric shelves
microwave
full basement

laundry
garage
rec room
electric broom
1 pussy
or 2

bedroom
almond kitchen
carpet
blue
raspberry
beige
garden white
right

    booms thunders claps
    grabs pulls shoots
    bends

    sweeps cooks sucks
    shops drives mops
    washes mends

rubs back
keeps hands off
thermostat

knows when to
disappear

3/discount

snap crackle pop
pussy
born to serve
born to serve

snap crackle pop
pussy
born to serve
born to serve

yes thank you
3 and
1 vibrator
keep the change
born to serve

911

ring them up
ready or not
here I
come
eardrum
condom
ram rectum
underarm

born to serve
born to serve

rush
thrush
yeast
raw
microstat
monostat

vaginitus smegma
papaya pussy
torn
snap valium
crack
nerve
nerve
nerve
sneeze sperm
squeeze
pop
squeeze
squeeze
squeeze
push
pop
11 lbs
12 ozs
born to serve
born to serve
born to serve
born to serve
born to serve

chaka zulu

on capitol hill
I run errands wearing
a blacktshirt
with gold africa map
i love and live
my african heritage
redgreengold cloth
greenred waistbeads
earthshoes anklechain
dredlocks
echoing the wind
I rush past peoples drug

a young brother
eggplant skin
head shaven clean
bulging muscles
in the neck and face
steps out to me

hey chaka
chaka zulu
you chaka zulu aint you

I hug mypursecloser
I wear my home
onmychest
onmywaist
onmyhips
myankles myfeet
onmylips

but I am not
chakazulu

my brother in america
don't want me reminding him
how he don't want to be
no african like he look like me

my brother in america
thinks he's an american
thinks because he lives
in america he's an american

why if he is an american
somebody who looks like him
could forge a campaign for president
and may the best man win

but an american the color eggplant
cannot live in the white house
there will be no nontraditional
casting for the role of chief executive

I bumpintomybrother

I chisel
chaka zulu eyes
into his clean
shaven head

Aftermath

Black umbrellas
choreographed
under
rainsheets
neon reflections
on wet pavement
darting between
mangled cars
jammed horns
I am alone in
this accidental
travesty
a marriage
the noise tears
my temples
blood rushes from
my nostrils
I use my
pantyhose
to sop the
bleeding
I am late
for the divorce
and cannot stop
the bleeding.

the wail

lungs are caves where grief is stored
I release I release I release

poems attack me
in my sleep   I reach for a
pen to stab nightmares

two sisters

two sisters
mental health models
opinions sought as
community leaders
exchange faces
warn

blackwomen
keep silent about
abuses inflicted
by black men
for colored girls
the color purple
portray negative
black men

two sisters
mental health models
opinions sought as
community leaders
exchange faces
warn

blackwomen
be victims/martyrs
be tough as christ
blackmen
must have someplace
to slam frustrations
caused by racist society

two sisters
mental health models
opinions sought as
community leaders
exchange faces
warn

blackwomen's
sexuality
for colored girls
the color purple

myth of the superwoman
too pro woman
proper women
lavish attention
on their men

two sisters
mental health models
opinions sought as
community leaders
exchange faces
for

reasons
battered
beyond
reason

Ingrid

1
Ingrid lay
beneath the tulipbed
bullet holes shattered
her pretty head
spattered her to
bits on paisley
patterned walls
her daughters
her friends
slaughtered in
upstairs bedroom

2

a police woman
singer poet
mother
artist children
forgotten
excused to death

3

a private inquisition
a dignified murder
simple chattel
a wife witch
lilysoft
butchered
a consequence
a pulse paralyzed
agile bullets
comfort a
raging husband
a forsale sign
on the front lawn
coldwell realtors

4

the dead
are not dead
when they are dead
unjustly
a shadow wakes
a stomach quakes
blood rushes
to find
another house
to finish its
business

The Girls

D Street Women's Shelter poetry performance

1

Pamela floats like a black
crane   neck long hair
cornrowed elegant patterns

she wears a tall black
choir robe gold red orange
stole   bible open

knows she is saved
stands so that her presence
is not overlooked

her robe, her shelter

2

Cheryl soft like dyed
brown cotton soft like
shedding dog fur voice

hushed eyes pleading
for her space her
moment of recognition

once wrote short stories
wrote poems once couldn't
carry everything with her

when she left.

3

Alice was a dancer
must have once danced
with the american ballet

theatre   a weathered
barbie doll aged agile alive
she talked about theatre

improvisations asked the
girls to get behind the
feelings in each poem

she wanted respect

4

The women entered me
through worried worn seat
covers like wolves howling

insane   they entered me
through shit pasted floors
pee dripping from walls

they entered pounding
multiple fists in my chest
eyes screaming/whispering

I was their solid oak door

Songbird's Abortion

Only once is sacred
when the choice
is clearly
hers

But he decides

he tucks her feet
behind her ears
reaches
his furry paw
inside her vagina
clasps the miniature
light in his fist
yanks the umbilical
cord claims it
as his own
sweeps the untimely
mess from his shoes
again
and again
and again

Only once would I
arch my throat
to utter a silent
wail fear trembling
limbs and trills
no more
give up
for an ungodly
power to play godlife
goddeath his belly rolling
thunder threatening
flash and fire

Only once would I play
the fool and fowl
allow
the mighty shaking
of godboy

to capture
silver joy
my bluejay bell
in his naughty fist
and twist

Piece O Meat

flashing red light
piece o meat
strapped down

I'm reading 120 over 90
on the right

the head a gong
heavy and shrill

stop   lift   roll
wait   wait   wait
snot and tears blind
the air a corset

normal

wait   wait
piece o meat
bluecross/blueshield
no gain no pain

allstate
bolted down
wait   wait

Hey somebody get me outta here

wait   wait

rip neck out of vice

dance   you a dancer at your age
you better be glad to get back
to teaching that's the best I can
do for you

wait   wait

Hey   Hey   Hey You
Unstrap my legs
My back hurts in this position

I'm sorry but you'll have to

wait   wait   wait   wait

mam what does your back have
to do with your legs

ezekiel cried dem dry bones
now here the word of the lord
de leg bone connected to de

piece o meat

wheeled   pushed   poked
layed open
cowery shells snatched
from dreds
metal hands
scrape
demand meat
relax
disgusted
meat won't cooperate
with radio
active treatment

my back
I can hardly walk

dis   missed
softcollar
cane
medicine papers
bill

Poem at Fortythree

No one is fortythree
forty three times
maybe but not
fortythree
alone

a soft rain
waters my
lawn

frogs chant
reversals
to summer
the washing machine
hums

gladys knight
til I see you again
soothe my back

I stare at dolly
partons tits on tv
my hands ache
eyes drool

I am jealous of lovers
curled and kissing
on sunday night

glad I'm not
in the cast
of best little whorehouse
I wouldn't remember my lines
with dolly's chest on the set

I crawl to my
heating pad
alone

No one is fortythree
forty three times
maybe but not
fortythree

Paranoia

Of the millions of women
in the universe, she is
certain that her personal
business is neon sign worthy

New York Times front page
worthy like everybody
gives a damn about a black
woman's state of affairs.

Anyhow, paranoid or not it's
her business and it's important
for women not to put their
business in the street. So

She tucks hers away in poems
and stores them in cobwebbed
corners in boxes behind the
linen in the linen closet.

She has a particular friend
who has a key to go in and
remove the boxes in case she
has an automobile accident/dies.

Unlike radical feminists who
chant *the personal is political*
or the good poet who has mastered
the art of circumlocution, she

Thinks her business is to tell
the truth without telling a lie.
Not telling her business is lying
by omission but since it's

Important for women not to put
their business in the street
I've tucked hers in the
spaces between these lines.

in the belly

My God the light is blindingly painful!

For Rachel
and the FW3 Not-Mothers

Momma
the gap between your nipple
and the rigid pull of my tongue

A slender difference between
feeding my tender core

and a mother's masturbation
I am weaned

I ride the waves fanning
out to sea twisting my hair

sucking my tongue   I do not
drown   though I do not know you

I needed to swim safely
in your smell to stroke your

smooth brown face   rub my small
hands in the upsweep of your

hair   I needed to hear the
stories behind your eyelashes

I need to pat your belly-
button roll my head

in your soft section be
squashed in your folds

now I sing a howling soprano
a calf in a pasture of silk

where hunger moves continuous
humps and ridges through my ribs

wanting intercourse with the
sun and sea and sand

I give birth to myself
I call every woman mother

real women

1
burgeoning breast
menses flow atlantic
two
teen-agers
shatter
tranquil hours
mom
something red is all
in my underpants at
age 12 and quieter at
age 19 *mom I need some*
money for birth control
pills
I am not ready to mother
women

2

the oldest one
chose a horn player for
her boyfriend
the youngest kept
hers hidden in
letters snapshots
I remember one christmas
she asked *mom am I old*
enough to date? I wanna
go to the movies with
poochie and gus all
I heard was two
two boys at one time
my voice cut
like a double-edged
razor
where are they
timidly she pleaded
mom you're
lookin at em

3

the unending tapestry
of cords connecting
hair blowers electric
curling irons
hairdye stained towels
hairperm stained table cloths
hair conditioners
mirrors booked two days
in advance for elbows bent
at forty-five degree angles
crimping, cutting, rolling
lambs wool which must be long
on one side cut above the
ear on the other
makes me wonder if
they like themselves

4

the mystery of
teens toilet paper
and towels
is like
alfred hitchcock's
missing leg of lamb
one roll of toilet paper
per day per teen
a labyrinth of beach towels
bath towels hand towels
dish towels
from bathroom to
bedroom
a. either they are anorexic
and chew toilet paper
to keep from eating or
b. they're full of shit or
c. they plan to surprise
me with a terry cloth
quilt for christmas

5

teen-age minds are rapid
transit systems they go
from hopscotch to jack daniels
and back again in minutes
at home
they sleep with
stuffed fuzzy animals
mammoth posters of
hottest jock singers
on walls
away from home
wine coolers are in
loud laughter/talk
in a language known
only to the relevant
"word" "girlfriend"
"yo" "stupid"
"why you dissin?"
rhythm/bass of
anita baker salt n pepa
pump from the ground
through the roof
to prove they
are real women
they must wear my clothes/
drive a stick shift car
never automatic
automatics are
fraudulent

6

they take music
fortissimo tv double
forté hair styles boys
unkempt surroundings
my choice classical jazz
natural hair silk flowers
muted tones
hushed surroundings

I am moon
rubbing night between
palms to make
muses sing
they are sharp
blades of sun
shooting through
my heart   they
make me warm
make me crazy
make me soft
make me silly
make me grow

Prelude

winter solstice

When winter comes
the tree sleeps dead

its branches dry and brittle
the loose bark hangs damp

a purple brown thing
near a glass pond where

mallards freeze on this blue day

I snap the dead branches
first her each finger   snap

then each one of her toes
every winter a new woman breaks

now I break the dead bones in
stark day of frost where want

and need burn the same where who
loves best becomes least loved   where

oh where has my little girl gone
oh where oh where can she be

Fugue 1

where once your coaleyes strummed
a metal heart   knight in white

advance a king's mouth   retreat
baby-milk breath

where once your sun-face spilled
over beet-red roots your book-laughter

dug trenches in whistling wind
sang my skin cellos

where once we half-slept in different
shoes   heels run over the same

bellies full of daffodils
picket signs purple pansies

you cast a single wire from asia
to africa to america

uncoil electric tongue strike
eyes white ignite pages torn from

the old testament   hot as iron your
words fuck the music from my third

chakra if I wanted to love a blackone
I would

I vomit ice
scream a hurricane

blow you back
to nest in winter solstice

Fugue 2

Summer's black lily
will not finger fresh gardens

On shadowy streets she will
loosen spider trapped in concrete games

Games that float in and out of season
heavier than snowdrifts that bury naked limbs

Lighter than spring rains that
drum out new breaths

Now you see me now you don't
I love you I hate you no you won't

No I won't yes I am not here I'm over
there touch me see I'm still not here

Take it slow I guess I mean to mend
my web tomorrow's pleasure please

Do not go I just don't know I'm
spinning now see please go slow no

Summer's black lily
will not finger fresh gardens

Mudpuddles for mirrors
she will strut and pose

And pluck spider's bluesharp
fresh fingers trapped

the ballet
as it was in the beginning

rise up Sun
dance your ascent
turn up from
the valley
present

first position
attitude
plié and
rise

over hills
wildflowers
over lakes
over meadows
pine trees

and
one two three
grand jeté relevé
and bend
my friend

wind oh wind

did you call
my name

did you clap
my face

are you pulling
me out of
the wood

I am earth
brown redrich

come
daughter
let me touch you

cradle my fragmented
head

nuclear distress

protect my
brown eyes
ah Sun

chills
I am ill

come daughter
speak

ozone seeps

hold my clay
as I have sustained you

the blowing of rock
the blasting of green

the solid is finished

A woman

we gather here in vapor
to mourn the passing of
our dear mother

we the ocean the trees the birds
the pigs and sheep

A woman

she fought a long and
tedious battle against man's
invasion of her interior

she gave to all who inhaled
her greens and blues suckled
her browns

A woman

as we commune here in nothingness
we mourn our nonexistence
celebrate our triumph over
man

A woman

Sun gone
down
dance your descent
chainés turn*
chassé
sissonne
échappé
and
lift
mist
vapor
void

chainés/she-nay
chassé/sha-say
échappé/aye-sha-pay

harmony

birdie go home, birdie go home

zora

in boiling sun
i look among the weeds
of eatonville for you
who strutted hats
cocked and feathered
draped-down pants when
women knew their
places

most townspeople
never heard of you
i pronounce your name
more deliberately
z o r a n e a l e
h u r s t o n
hunted
jook joints
of mississippi
for the souls
of her people

a dusty finger
points out your
house among a dull
row of shanties
the one with the
sanctified screen door
crying on dried hinges

in boiling sun
i search the
splintered wood
the taller brush
for your stone
the one alice
had engraved
a genius of the south

i want to break bread
drink wine
with you who

spit back hell from
the niggerati
your brazen tongue
died cold in hand

a charge to keep i have
a god to glorify
who gave her sun
my soul to save
and fitted for the sky

by half moon
i turn graves
to find your
oyster knife
suspended between
my thighs

Needs 1986

I have never met
ronald reagan
slippery cracked
porcelain cowboy
barbedwire
deciduous smile
I have more
immediate needs   like
finding an affordable
house a tax shelter
buying fresh fruit and
vegetables conscious
of stealing from farmers
who cannot get loans to
feed america.

I have never been to
tripoli or managua
when washington is
capital of the world
managua
a country club for
american diplomats
air bases in honduras
smithsonian museums
and tripoli
another disney world
where the mad dog
is the meanest
roller coaster on the planet.

I have not even
seen big mountain
the diné and hopi
peoples are crosses
ground into lithium
because it is cheaper
to mine sovereign
indigenous people
than to acknowledge
their needs.

My world is more
immediate   close to
the white house
close to compulsory
urinalysis   drug testing
for workers
except marion barry
merit pay for teachers
who believe in exploitation
close to
tracks and p street beach *
fag bashing and aids victims
left to die because
sodomy is against the law
mouth to genitals
genitals to anus
which means tribadism
is legal.

And philadelphia goode
is part of the
good ole whiteboy
network   fascist
fundamentalist
m o v e murderer
while barry's back
stays wet with dogshit
where the homeless
crawl for recognition

My world is more
immediate
I have to tie up
sprouting dreadlocks
to keep p g county police
and the caribbean cruise
foot out of my front door
I have to pay
for the washington post
for war mongrels
for heavy duty rehnquists
and meeses and scalias
who don black robes
in daylight

white hoods at midnight
to the tune of yankee doodle
and I do do without
gold and diamonds
which is why I can
not remarry
and why I can
not eat meat
who can know that
ground beef is not a
chopped mayisa corpse
death squads fresh
catch-of-the-day
shipped from
south africa or
freeze dried ethiopians
capitalism is a euphemism
for cannibalism and
almighty God is the
F1-11 Bomber!

I have never met
ronald reagan
slippery cracked
porcelain cowboy
barbedwire deciduous
smile
my needs are more
immediate
I have to kill roaches
and stop people from
calling me
whoopie goldberg.

* gay club and park in DC

I Wanna Write

for Simone Zagore

I wanna write
a good poem
about a black man

I wanna write
about how this
boeing 747 bicep-bound
paul robeson-basso-profundo
saved his
woolyheaded charcoalwoman
how he
rolled her
in his dreams
about
goin to africa
to build a new life
for a new black people

I wanna write
about this divine man
who told the
capitalist mothafucker
to take its filthy hands
off his dignity
to piss on its
affirmative action
O E O—me and my
broadnose
watermelonlip woman
is goin home
FOR GOOD
to reclaim what is ours
what was our great great
great grandparents

We gon backstroke
to the mainland of
greenblackgold
and leave the
redwhiteblue
to the white
red
and blue you
yeah Blue
you gon be blue
when ain't no mo
niggahs
to take care of you
yeah
cause we takin
nell carter too!

Now What You Gon Do

SUCKER!

We gon take
all the black
outta white
we gon make
ourselves slaves
to freedom
no mo
softsatin cushion
to prop yo hate on
no mo
cadillacs
to collect on
no mo
michael jacksons
to market
no mo
love labor

We gon take away
all yo ghettos
all yo prisons
and most of yo
state mental institutions
now whiteboys
you satisfied...?

TAKE THE GOTDAMNED COUNTRY
WE DON WANT IT!!

We Built This Country
Under The Whip
Swingin From Magnolia Trees
just THINK
What We Could Build

free
from the kkk
free
from the fbi
free
from the cia
free
from mafia-white tv
free
from this land of greed
to hell with need
I wanna live
to write about
my man
takin his woman
home
for good.

Sixties

The sixties
our era to rage
now
after the purge
we ignore
racism

The eighties
a poem about race
is not a poem
people say   thats
sixties rhetoric
anger no longer
the correct response
to white supremacy

We put on grandboubas
not dashikis   dread our hair
no longer bushes call ourselves
kwekuhodarikunjufu
tote incense peddle oils
and vegetarian sermons
write safe poems about
trees in nicaragua cover
eyes with blue contact lenses
watch our sister host
forsyth county georgia on
national television
go back
tomm fetchit step
and be safe
the sixties was our
era to purge

Deny charred holes
in harlem watts
14th street dc
southeast
is a bantustan

glass chrome
granite marble
monuments to racism
rise from connecticut avenue

Forget
heads rolled off the tip
of hoover's tongue
forget
draft cards clogged sewers
so johnny could come marching home
peace be still
forget
james cleveland ordained
nikkigiovanni poet arsonist
forget
panthers parked rifles
between rightwing liberal eyes
police pigs broke many backs
broke no spirits
smash racism
jam the rubble down its
red white and blue throat
the sixties was our era
to rage

Remember
flames
shattering glass
tvs and stereos
running down city streets
remember
no forty acres
not one mule only
screams and uniformed
militia national guard
blank faces blocked
clenched fists angry
teeth *black power burn*
baby burn and water the water
tripping over water and fat
firehoses and more water

My water broke right after
the King was murdered
my daughter pushed fragile
and tightfisted against
walls of resistance

Maybe she will remember

the sermon

I dare to destroy ships then use the wreckage to build monuments of truth.

Rideon

I say righton

slave say rideon
talkin bout Jesus
doin his thing
tellin the pharisees
to kiss his ass
go head an put the
crown
on my head

sides bleedin
fingers numb
nailed feet blood
leather tongue
talkin in rhyme
slaughtered like
a hog

slave hogtied
hung out to dry
like Jesus beef
cottonpickin
back broke
yesuhmassuh from
frostbite in de
mornin til sun
stroke at night

I say
righton Garvey
righton Martin
righton Malcolm
righton Angela

Slave say
rideon Vesey
rideon Turner
rideon Tubman
rideon Kingjesus

Holy Man

for M.L.K.

We were graced by
a King whoes nappy
head would not

let him be called
the Messiah

Had to carry us
on your back
through the streets of
Atlanta, Birmingham
through the streets of
Montgomery, Selma, Memphis

A cross to bear

they laid you prone
naked on the waters

chernobyl/bhopal
leak in the mouth eyes become
anthill-seeing skulls

namibia

cinnamon fingers
strum mandolin eyes inside
namibian cage

jagged edges rip
bowels as slaves shit diamonds
to relieve pressure

afternoon grass shifts
tanks charge past okuvango
toward angola

one-arm ribcages
split like ripe watermelon
maggots salivate

children covet death
a ceremony   mint leaves
simmer holocaust

Sermon
The Holy Family

The holy family Well
garland hair, patent leather shoes
j&b scotch toast emerald green eyed
america in black face, the holy family
in ebony and essence. No errors
being black will never be forgiven. Sweetjesus

There is a flavor to reality that
is not profitable. The child beats
her mother with grandfather's cane,
the father generously toasts himself
inside his nine year old daughter,
Neither sells j&b nor essence.
Let the truth be quiet,
the tilted chin the smile pulled
back to tears pays more. Comeonupnow

What if grim laundry strung
across alleys' broken glass broken
children wrapped around absent mothers
lunatic fathers is a kind of perfection. Well

What if it is holier to take
reparations /welfare than
charge one's existence to visa or master card
and wait for the state to recognize
it's inhumanity. Well

What if the secret is in numbers,
how many we include from one rock
thrown in a muddy lake.
How far the ripples circle out
from brazil nut to haitian tan
russian coffee, namibian blue to
mozambique black
No throw backs,
from cracked plaster ceilings peeling
to stained glass shrubs
No give aways. The preacher and the prostitute
are first cousins, Watchyaselfnow

Bring back the bum curled on the grate — Hummmmmmmmm
my mother's brother, that junky is my father,
my lesbian sister who feeds the homeless
my son who died of aids, No dead give-aways
the politician, the pusher the
pregnant teen. The holy family. — Thankyoujesus

The roses are in bloom along
66 en route to Lorton. When we visit
relatives we will carry the fragrance
in the folds beneath our chin
between our cheeks and pray
we are not searched

Glory Glory
Hallelujah

the ringshout

I take back the drum   rhythm   sweet song my spirit flies

no history of
good love   shout the sky is not
always grey   Sun comes

love/war under the baobob

for Chuck Davis danceafrica'87

the Watusi is a
tank   a cannon
earth solid under
foot/song bells
call battle
right left right
left right left
left right left
right left right

balaphone and
kora weapons
tuned to
war without
bloodshed

under the baobob
griot bones
announce the plan

bamboo sistahs
sharpen rifles
one against the
other in rhythm
in time steppin up
tempo up tempo
time steppin thru
rain forest and
desert
they hoard bird
calls in gourds
to protect what is
sacred they drink
the music from the
gourd

drum hands drum feet
burn impressions
dancers leap/

writhe white
flame- shadows against
russet skies

a symphony of dark
bodies   swing battle
gun boots kick slap
shoot   reel   halt
begin again
shosh oloza
shosh oloza
right left right
left right
left right left
right left

the Watusi is a
tank   a cannon
mountains solid
under foot-
song bells
call love-war
for a
dangerous people

Sing A Softblack Poem

For Winnie Mandela

Sing a softblack poem
fora softblack sistah
to lay her head on

Winnie Mandela

sing blended sistahs
greenblue reddeeppink
drink from the same fountain
we hold the same cup
deep vibrations collect
around my spine
rocked in yo voice
with yo
shakere   tambourine
a liquid sugar poured
on my pain
a medicine to this
motha   sistah

terrorized at midnight
they bang on my door
throw stones on my window
my roof
blinded by torches
machine guns rifles
an army of afrikaners
to banish one bantu
woman

ring sweetharmonies
through raspberry lips
where is the pain?
tight brows
mid chest
slight throbbing temples
swollen ankles
acid gut

torn from Nelson Mandela
twentysix years
the pain is constant
humiliated harassed
tortured
strangled
lied on spied on spat on
detained under house arrest
thirsty for letters from Nelson
starved for family friends
I remain unbroken

Winnie

she talk if she want to
you just try you bloody cow
she move that band
she thump that shakere
like she thump apartheid
she not scared of nothin no more
political spiritual blues
walkin bass voice
walk them voices right
into Billie Bessie
Sarah blues
where is the pain?
nausea
blackwoman strong
but she be in pain

Sing a softblack poem fora
softblack sistah to lay her
head on

Nomzamo
Nomzamo Winnie Mandela
Nomzamo
Nomzamo Winnie Mandela

courageous
outspoken unbroken
rock me in yo circles
tie-dyed purpleorange

yellowgreen blue blended
range squeezed in the same
time blended where she
carries her babies she
carries her music she
carries her people
rich fertile womb
floods her lips

How can I lose hope
when I know
this country is ours

soblack

see

I am not white

I do not aspire to be
white

I work hard to stay
black

bold/italic/black
incense oil
burning candle black

I want to
think black
love black
taste black
teach black
bitchblack
inkblack

I want to pitch
my voice midnight
drumout my name

say I've known rivers *
instead of I pledge allegiance
sing god bless the chile
instead of america

I want to be rawblack

I want to be soblack
shacks grow out of my back
dandelion greens sprout
my eyes

I want to be bossblack
three-piece corporate image

nappy edges   grandbouba
briefcase   gutblack
gourmet
chitlin circuit
hamboneblack

I am a state of emergency

I want to be soblack
antjamimas n uncletoms

who say black black black
I'm sick of hearing it
loosen they bandanas when
they smell me coming

I want to be soblack
f b i taps my phone
cause they think I am
malcolm reincarnate

I want to be razorblack
get arrested for
slicin the moon into
three equal planets

ghetto
bantustan
reservation

I want to be screamingblack
so squad cars
screech to a halt when
I walk cross the street
I want to be sweet streetblack
so I am booked for
disturbing the peace

arrest me
arrest me

yes

I am a state of emergency

I am the
big butt
loud lip
loose hip
ret tittied
tambourine
shoutin
switchblade
cussin
aretha singin
lena lovin
momma

> *the*
> *boogie woogie*
> *rumble of a dream*
> *deferred**

arrest me
arrest me

I am the
oogha boogha
jungle bunny
voodoo mule
common
bare breasted
barc footed
dancing
licorice sweet
down
any street

I sing

I testify

I call

> *Ago ou we*
> *attibon legba*
> *ouvri bayé pou moin*
> *ouvri bayé* **

arrest me
arrest me

pleaze

* from Langston Hughes

** Vodun ceremonial song

Native of Cincinnati, Ohio, Kwelismith is a graduate of the Cincinnati Conservatory of Music. Now living in Washington, DC, a poet/singer, actress, dancer and music educator, she has a Masters Degree in Counseling Psychology and is the mother of two daughters. Kweli has performed her one woman shows, "When I Lay My Burden Down" and "Noplace Fora Softblack Woman" at The Kennedy Center, The Bethune Museum Archives, Sanctuary Theatre and the Smithsonian Anacostia Museum. She has also been a recipient of The Barbara Deming Award, The Institute for the Preservation of African-American Writer's Promotional Award and a DC Commission on the Arts and Humanities Fellowship Grant. This is her first collection of poems from 1984 to 1989.